THIS BOOK BELONGS TO :

Copyright © 2024

By Dr. Wayne Shuler II

All rights reserved.

No part of this book may be reproduced in any form or by any means without prior written permission from the copyright holder.

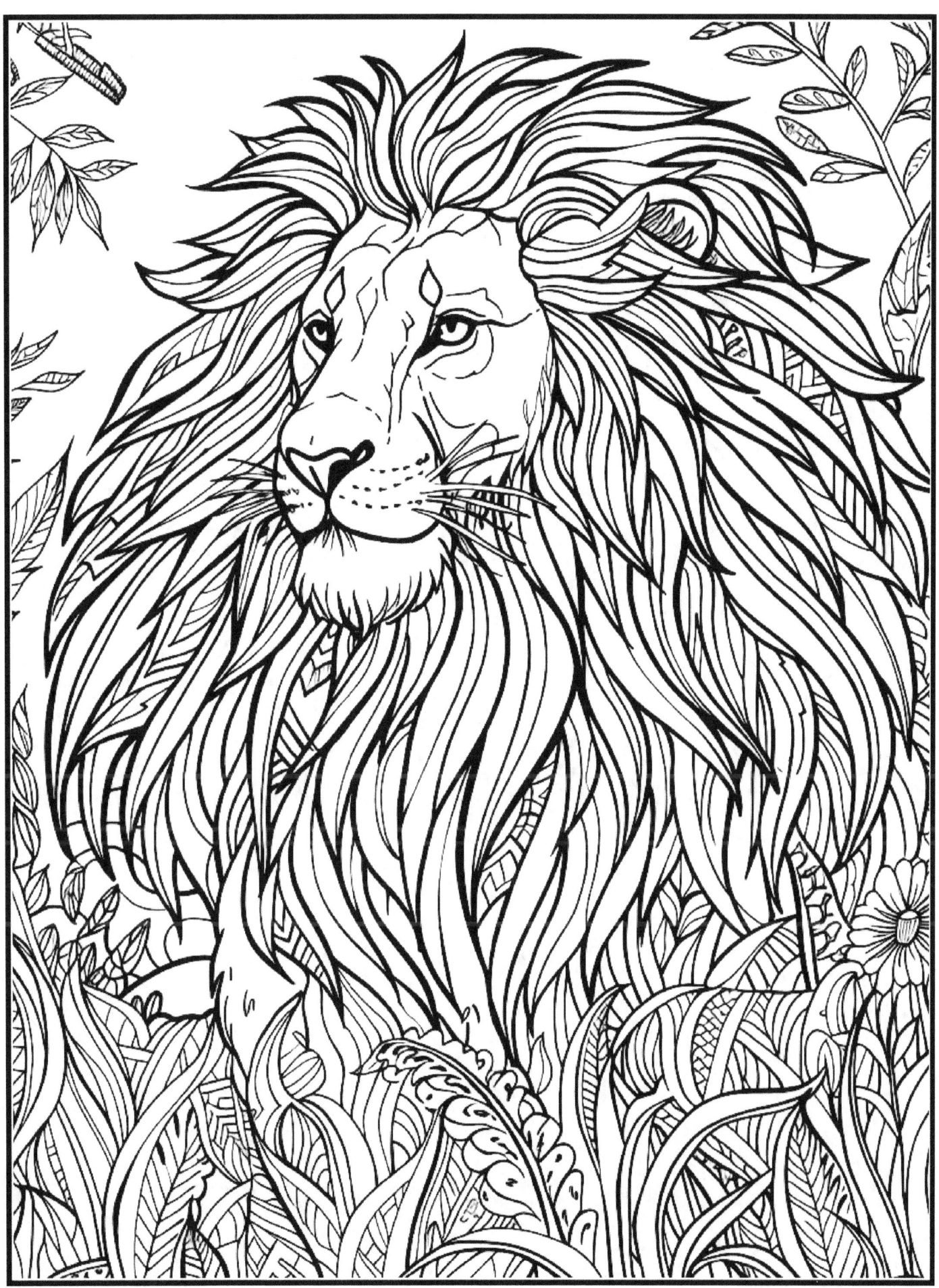

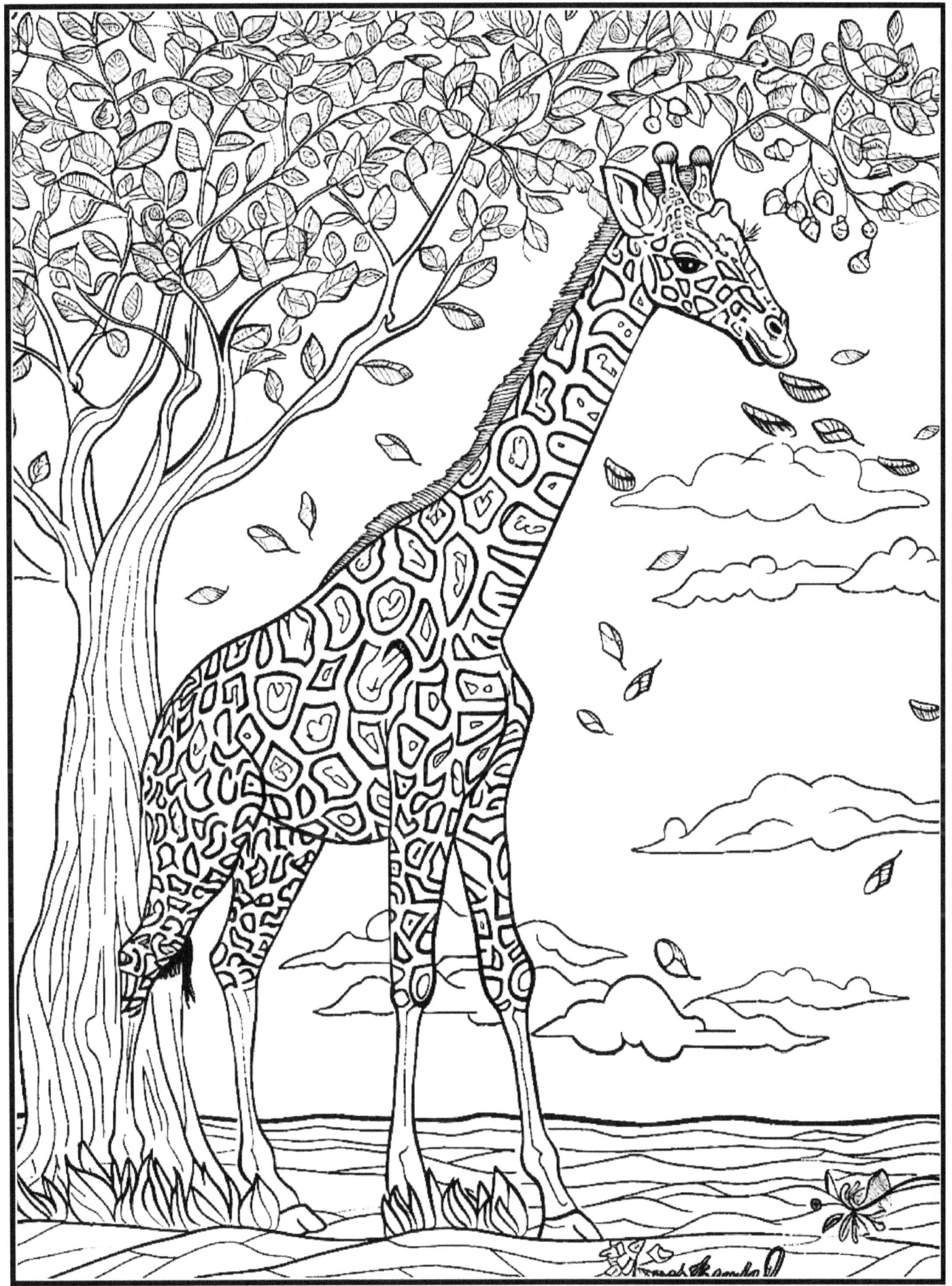

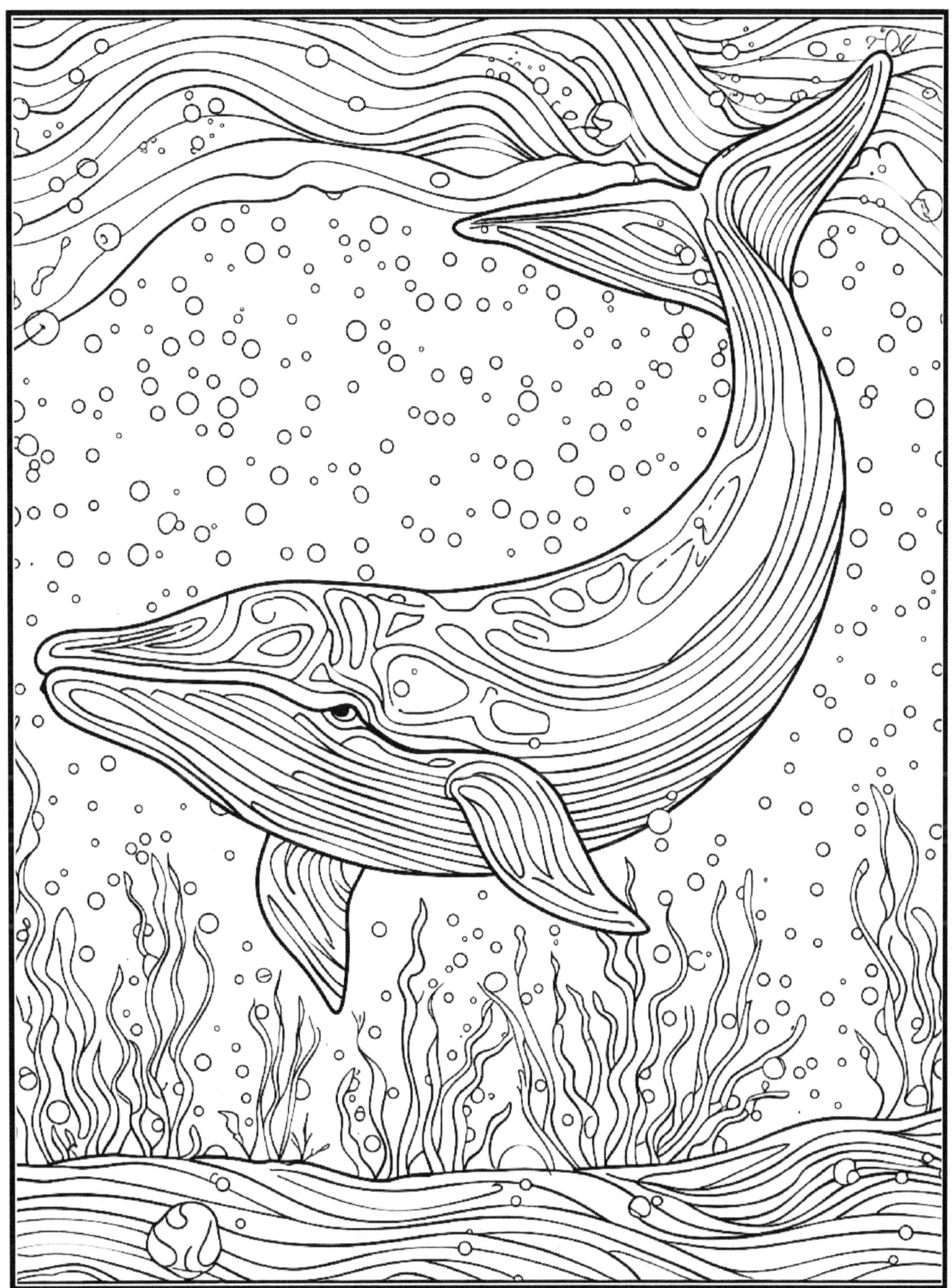

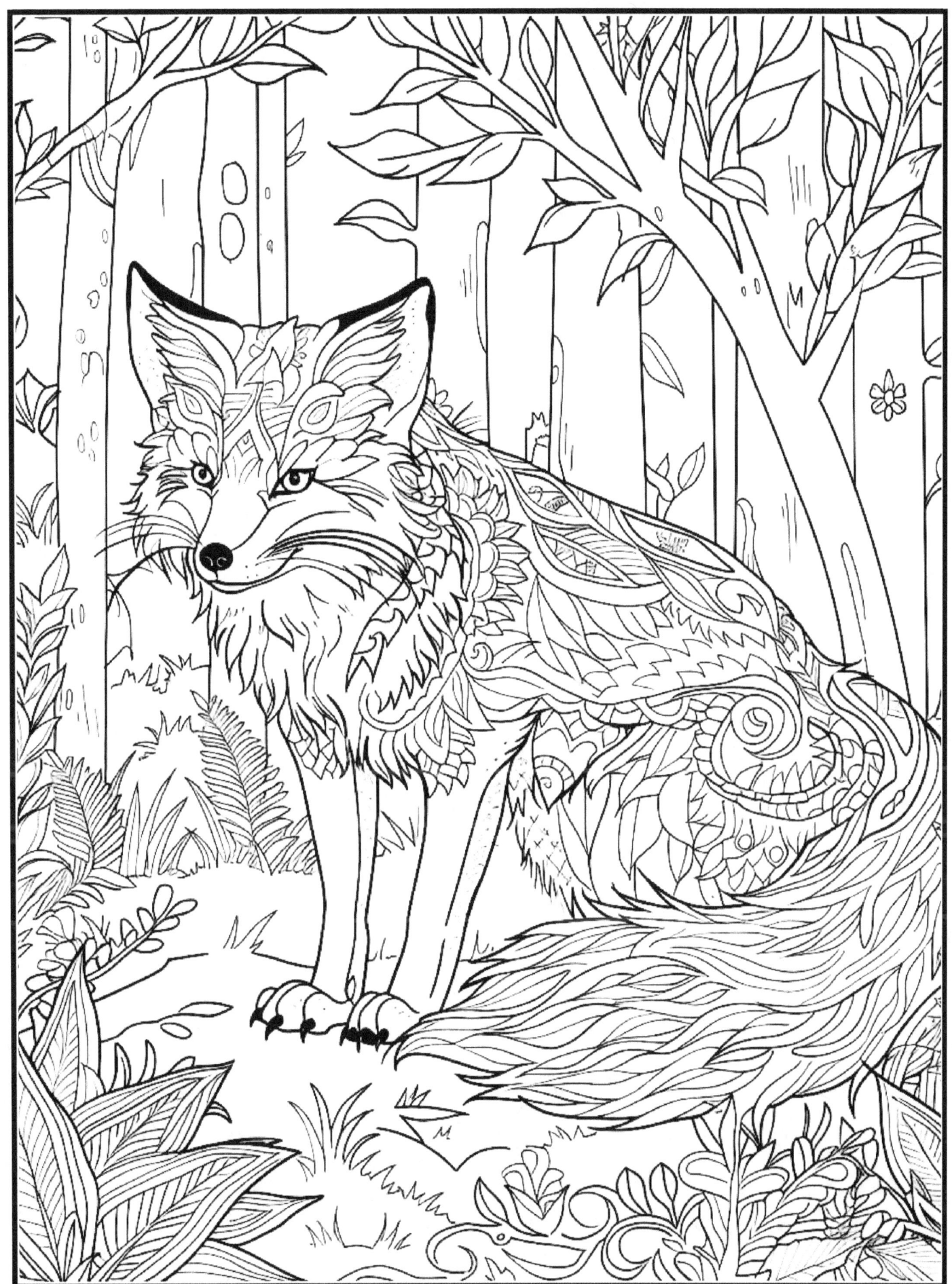

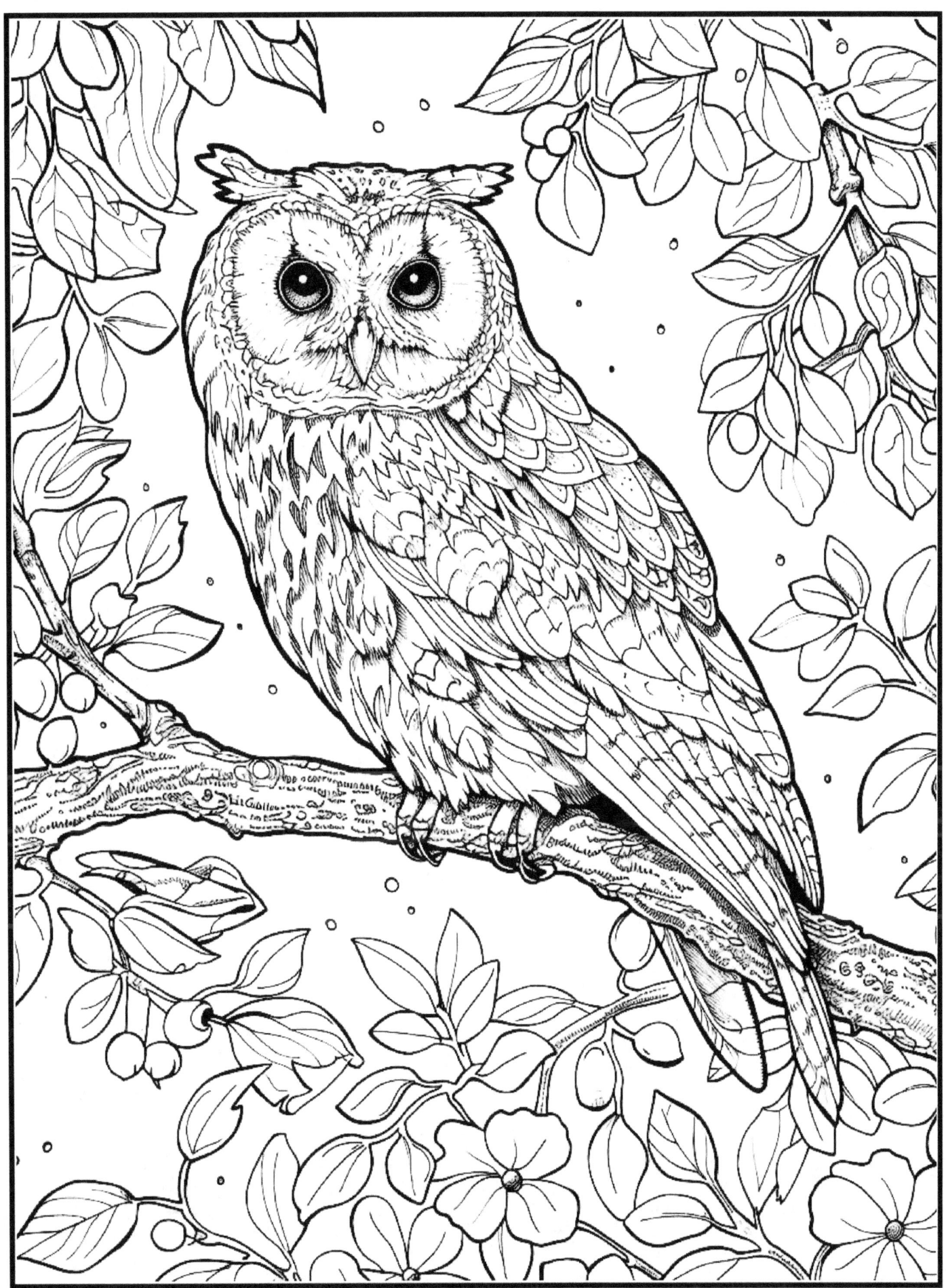

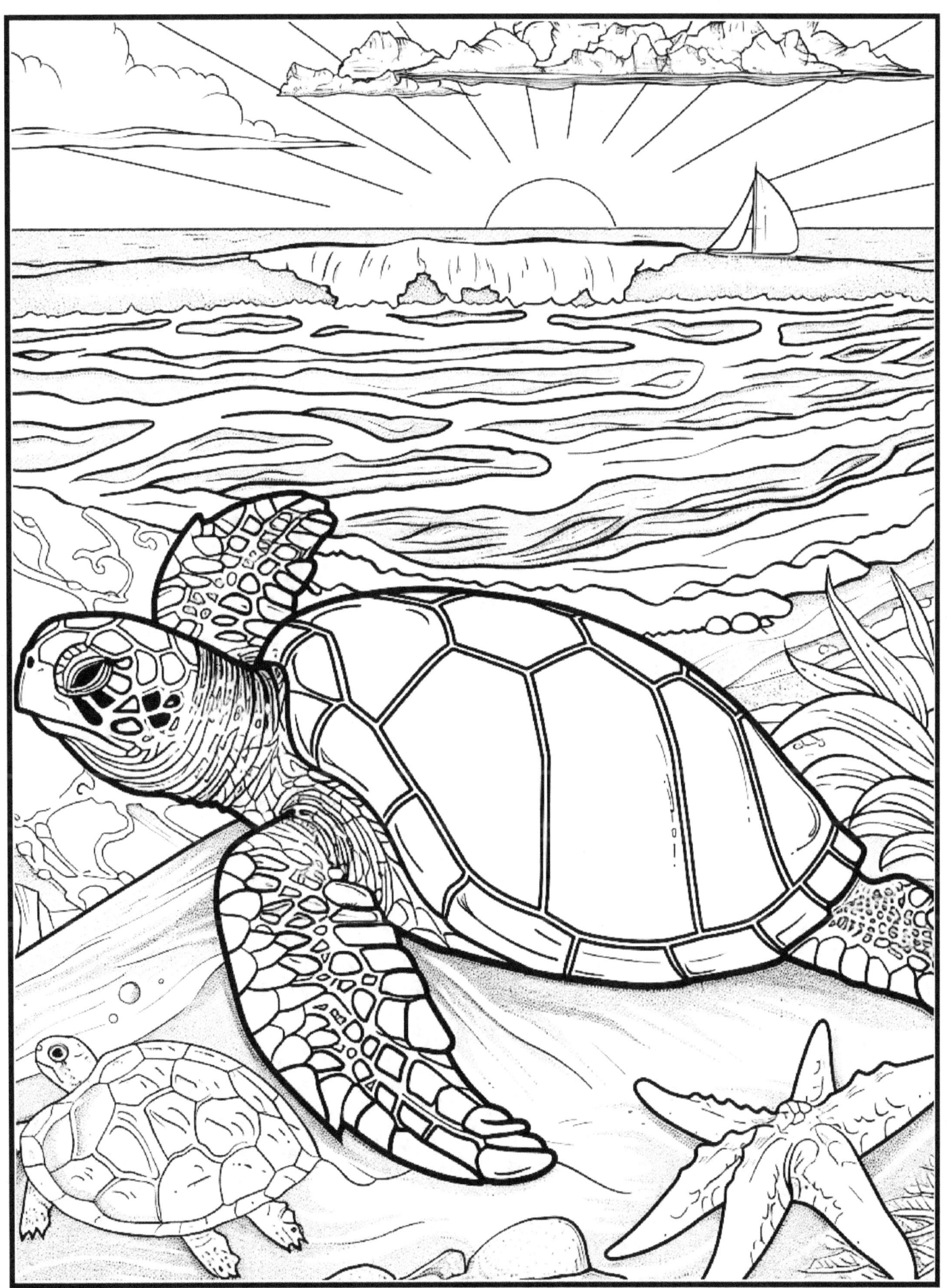

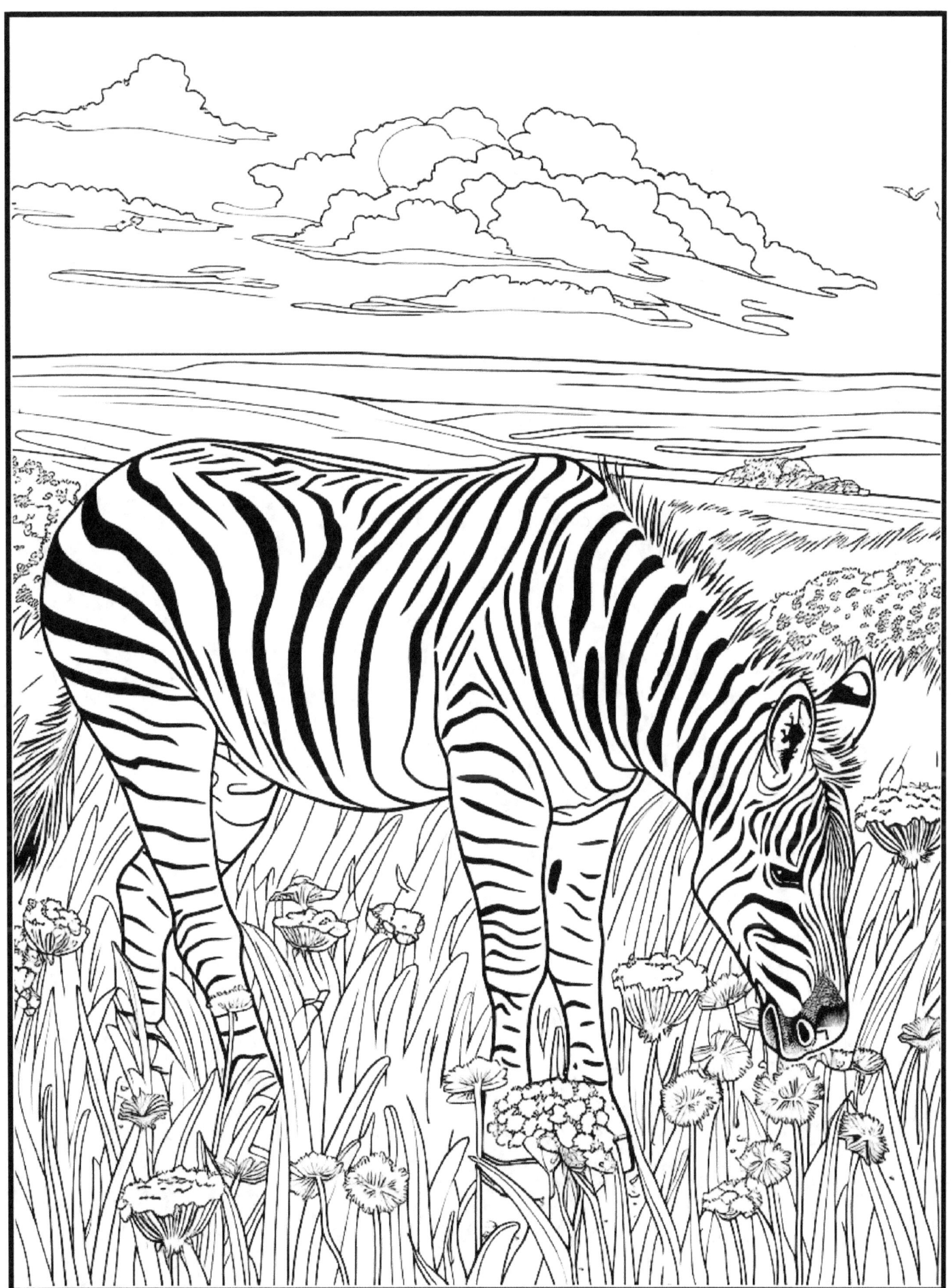

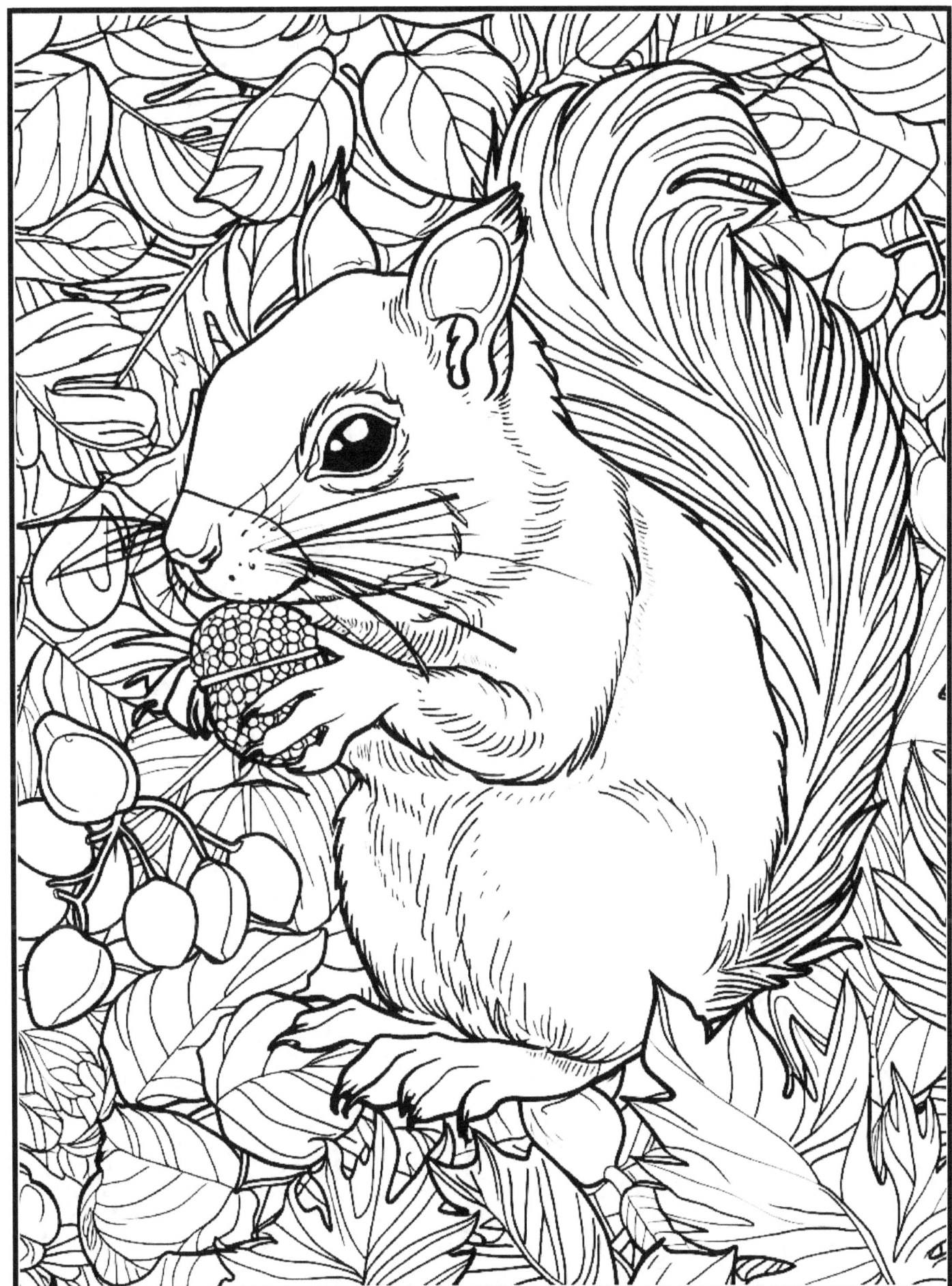

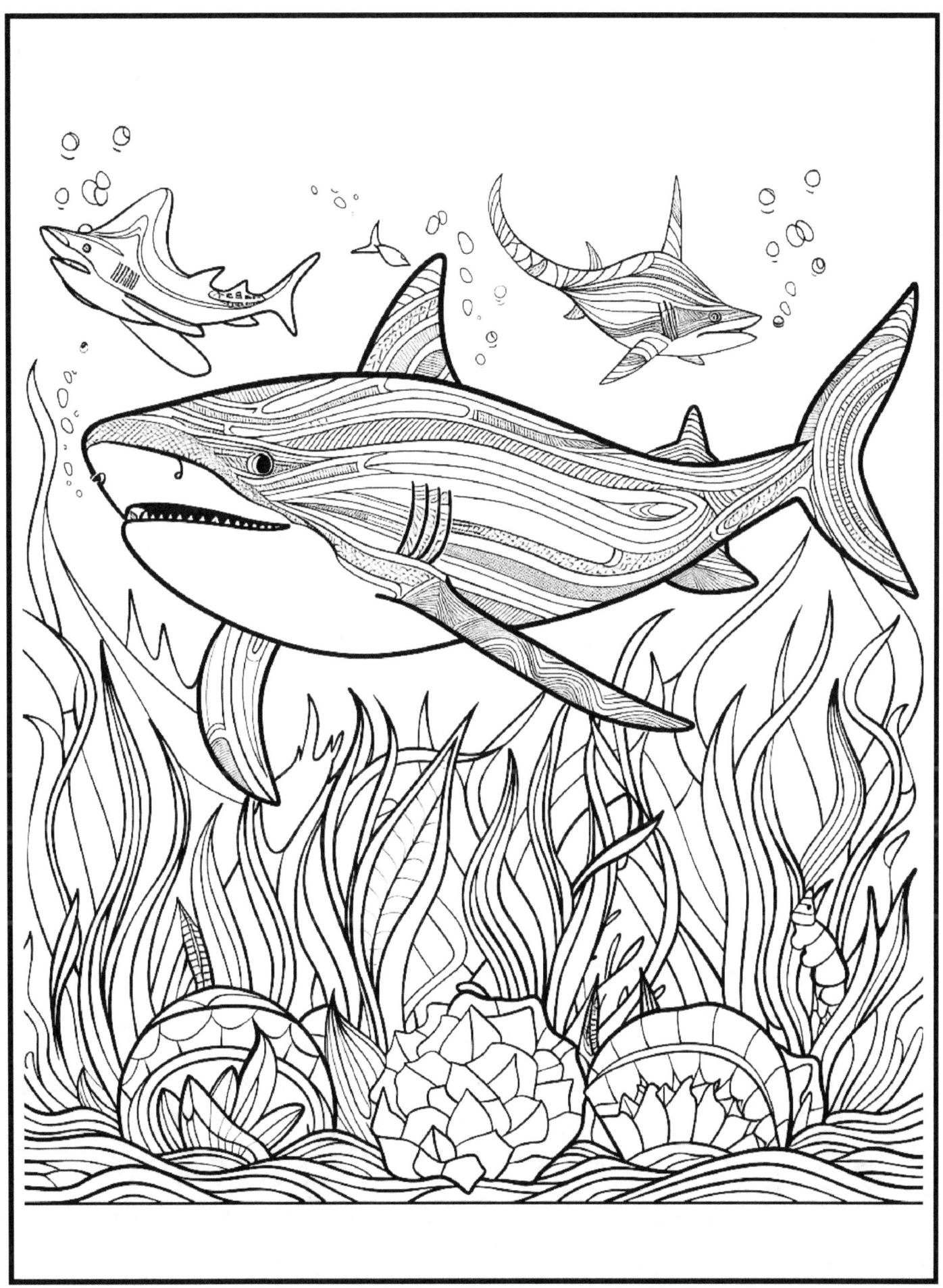

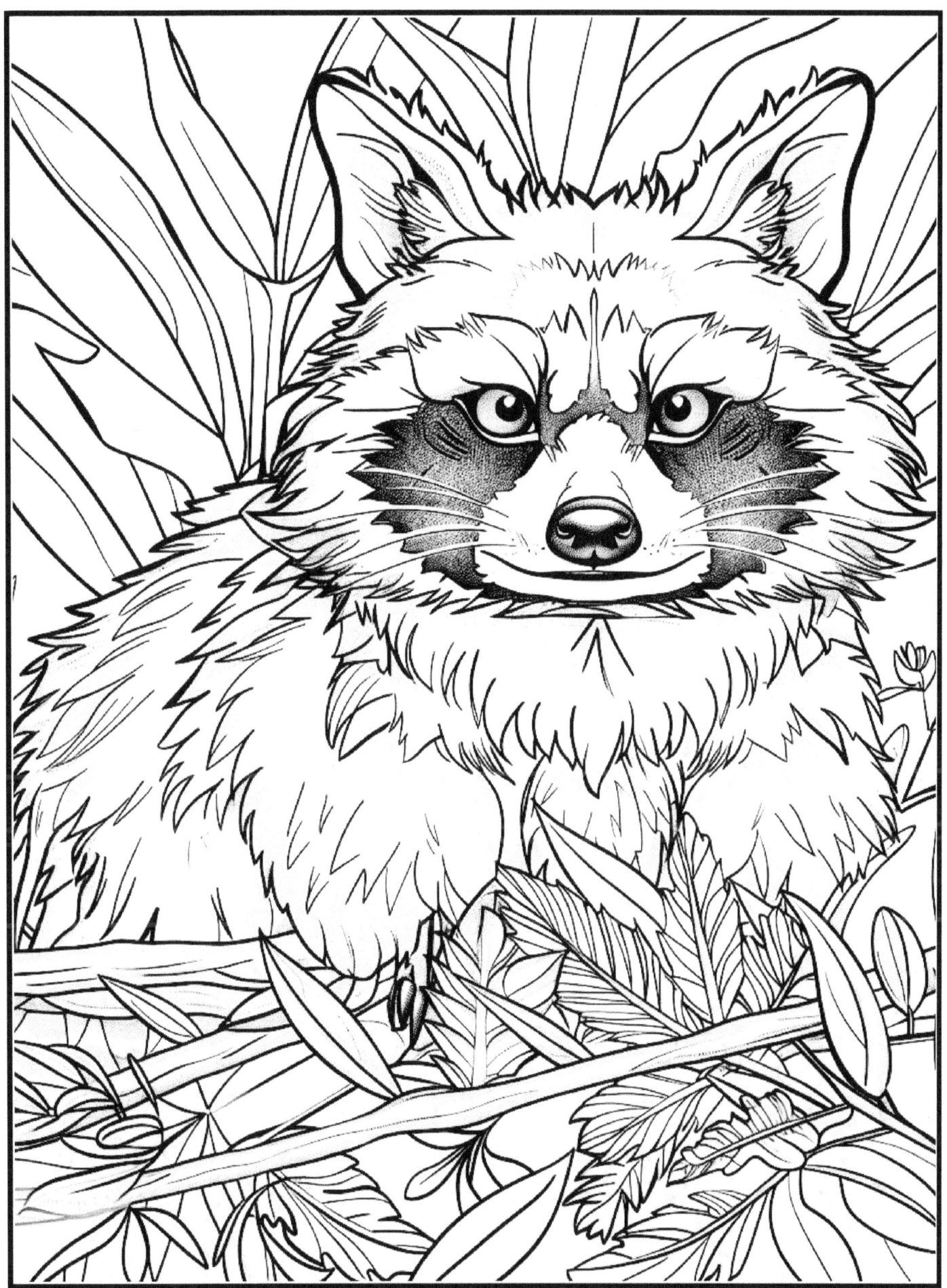

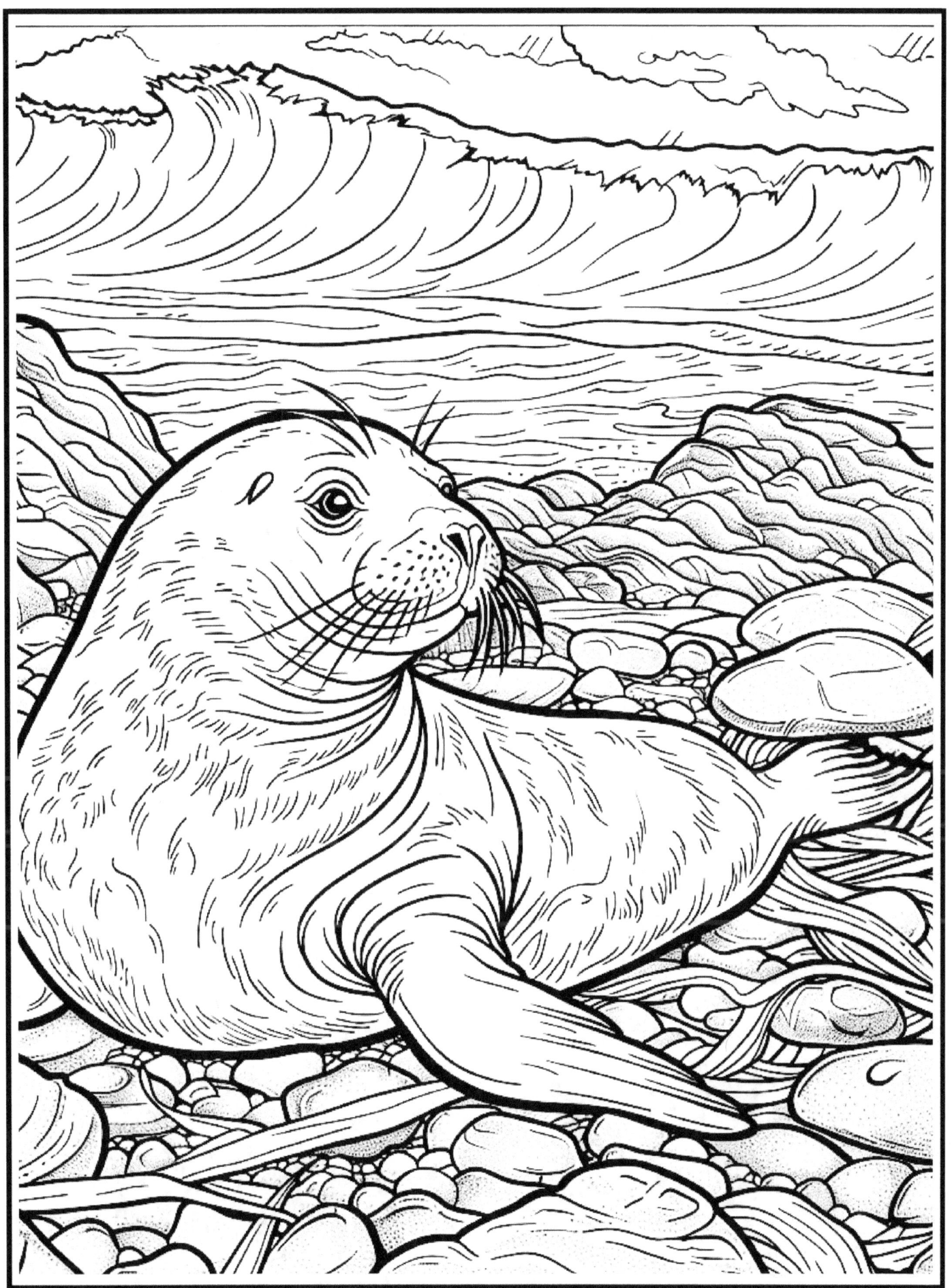

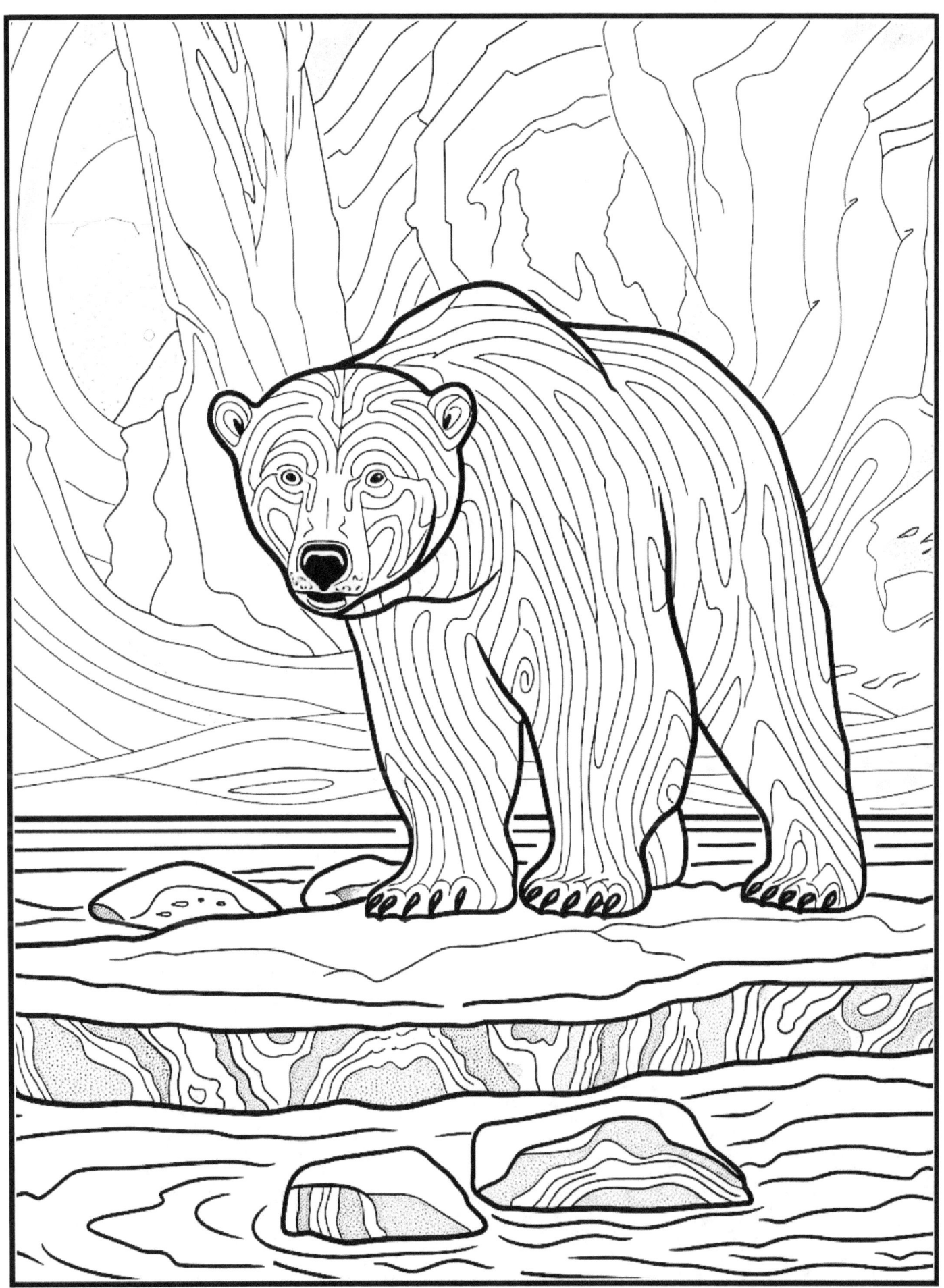

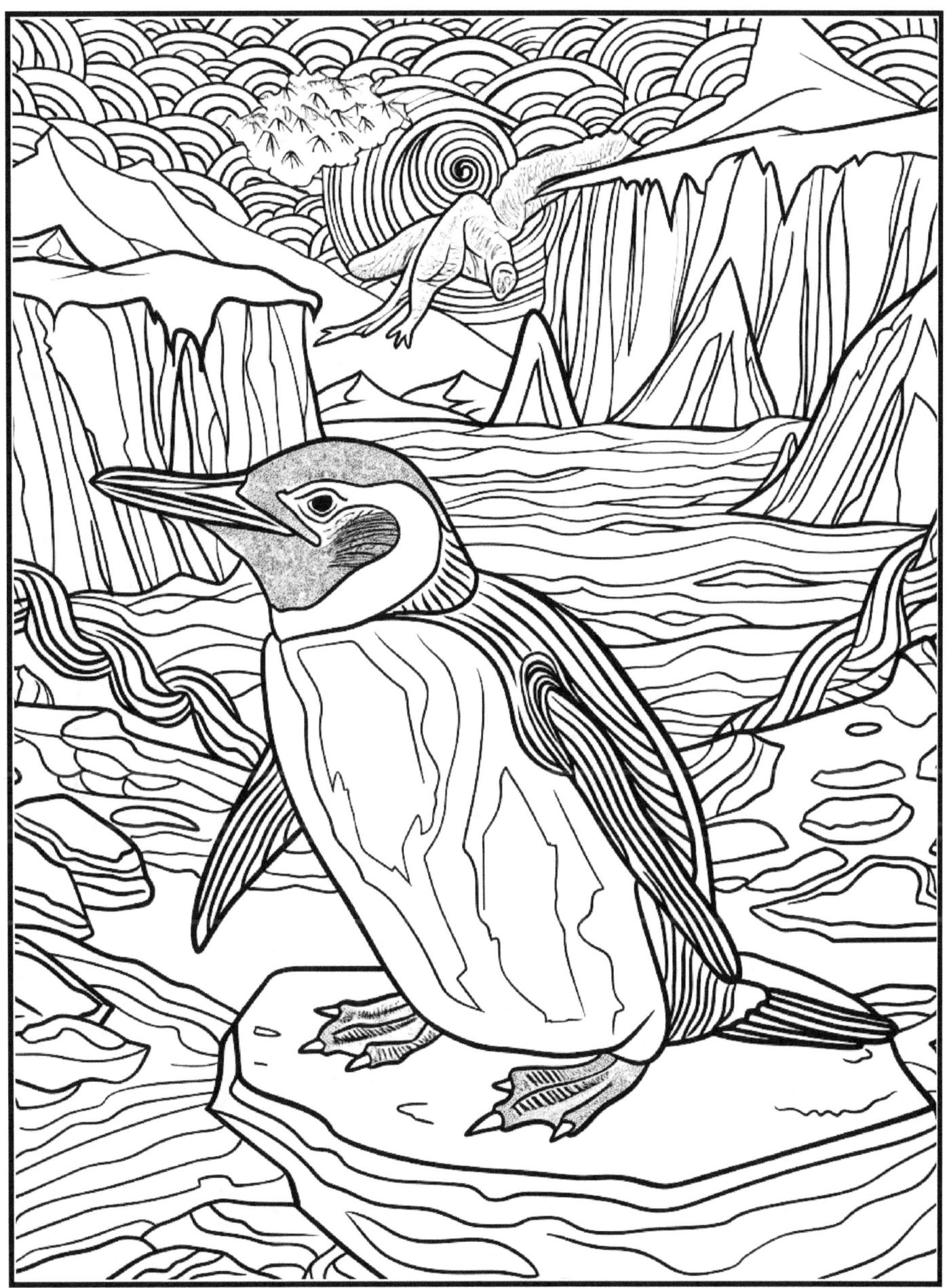

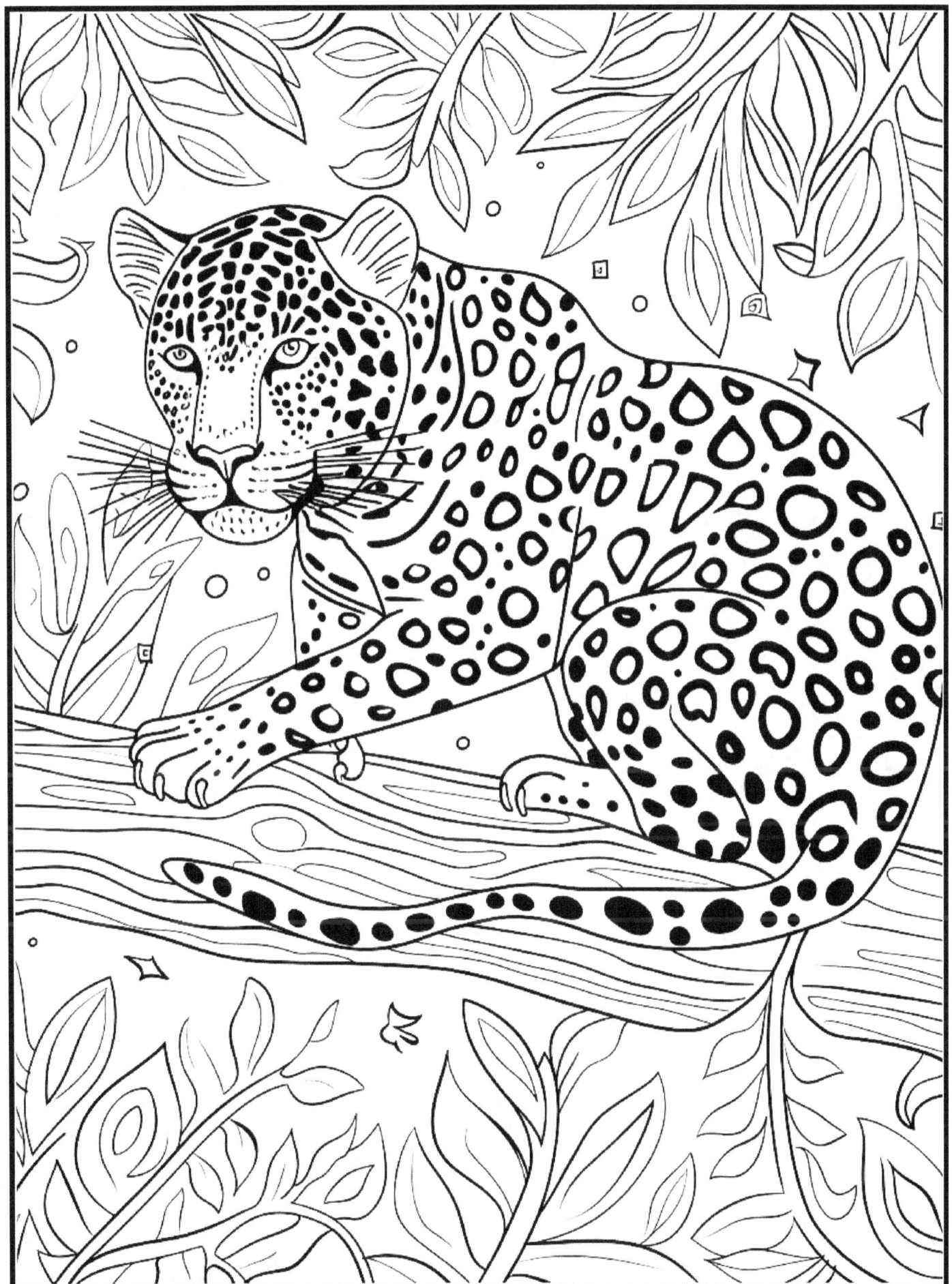

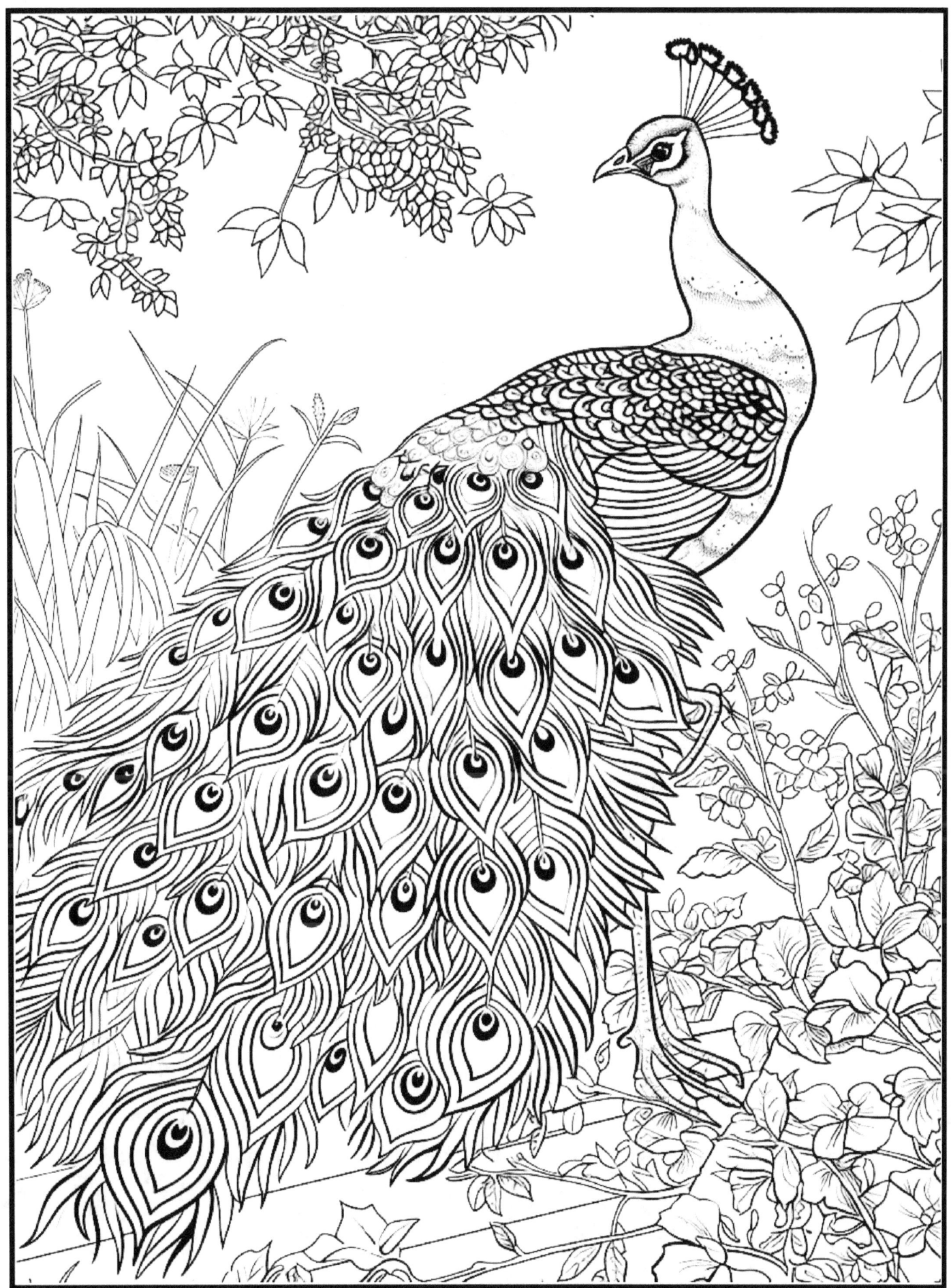

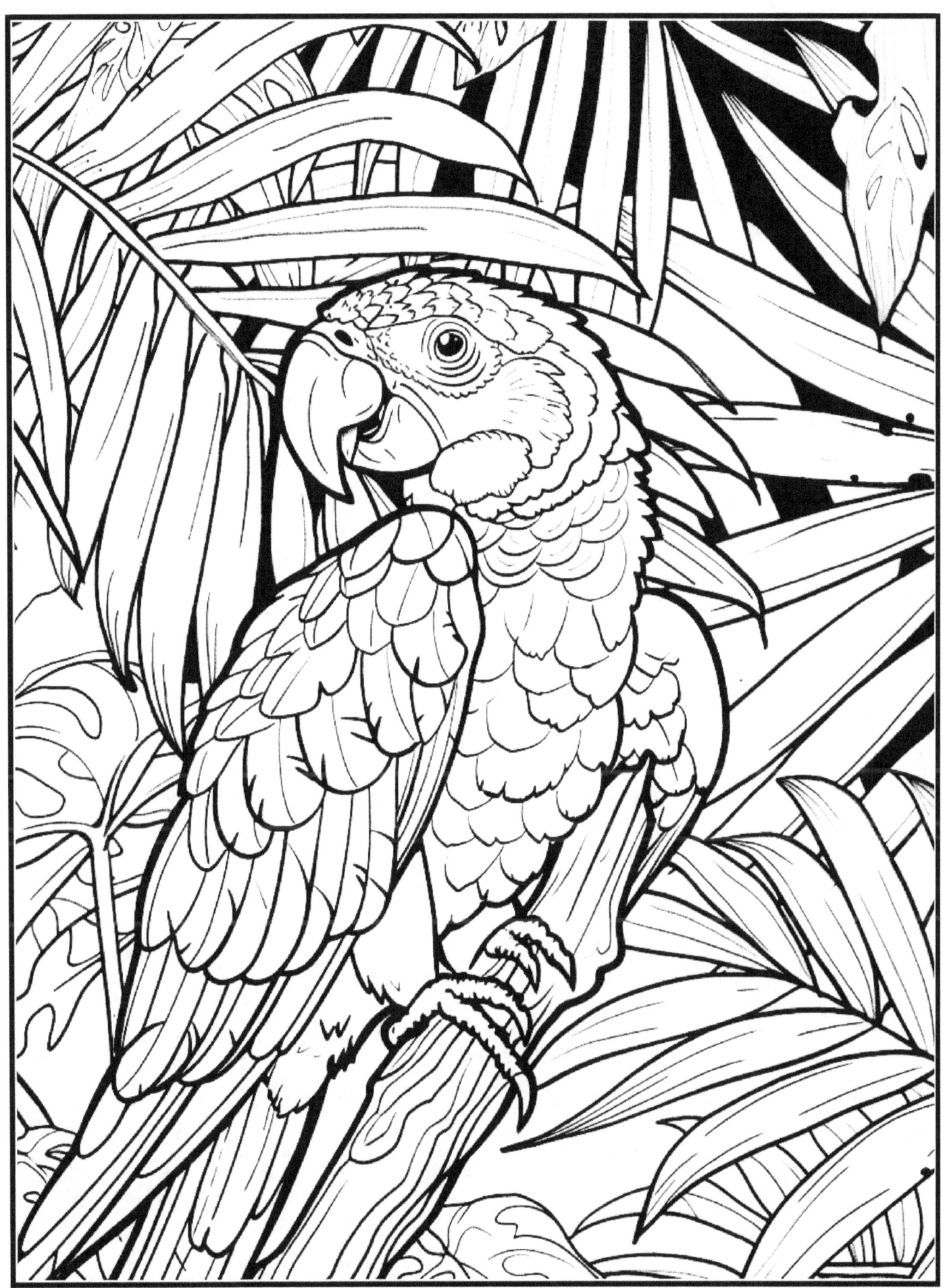

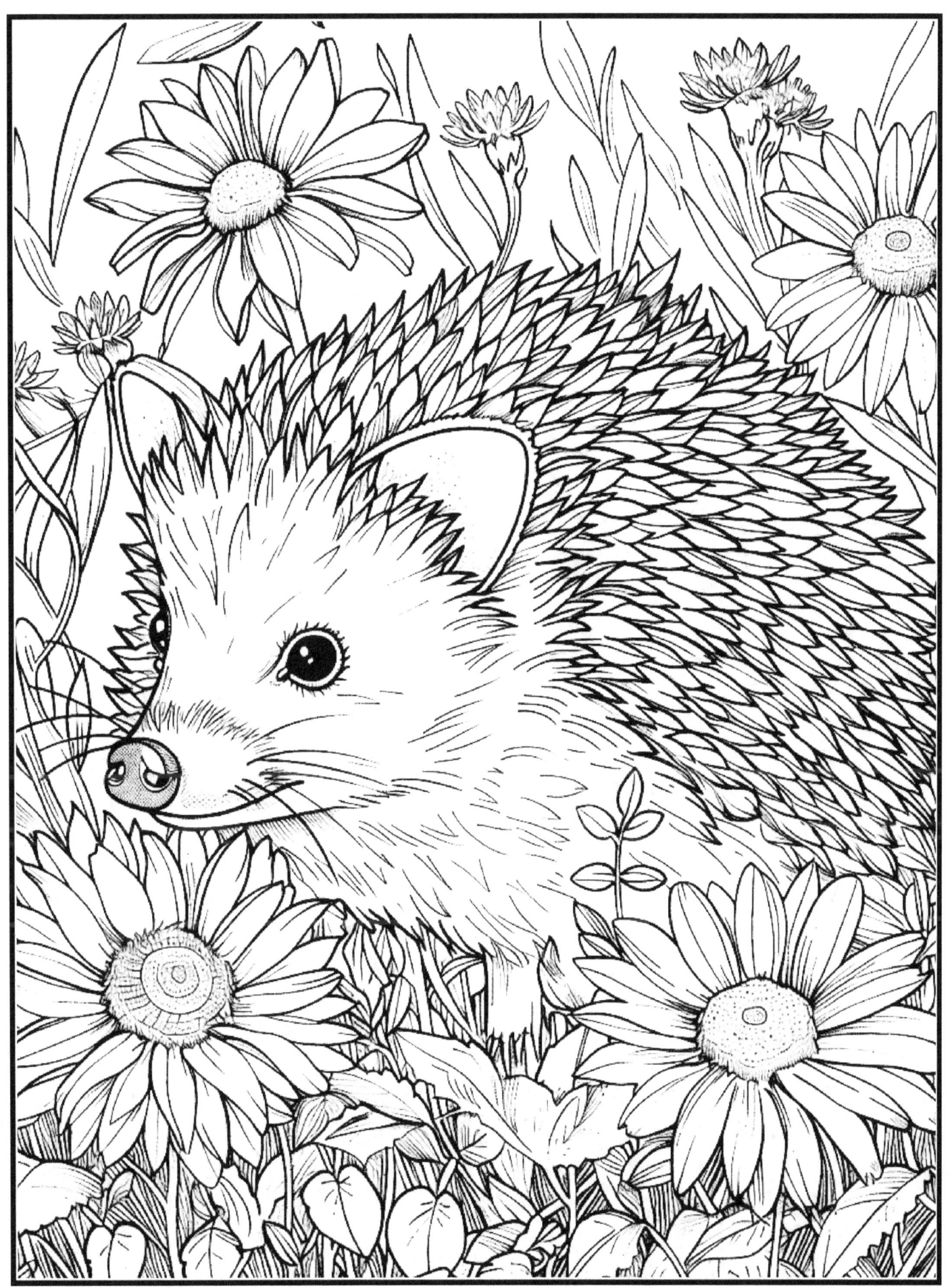

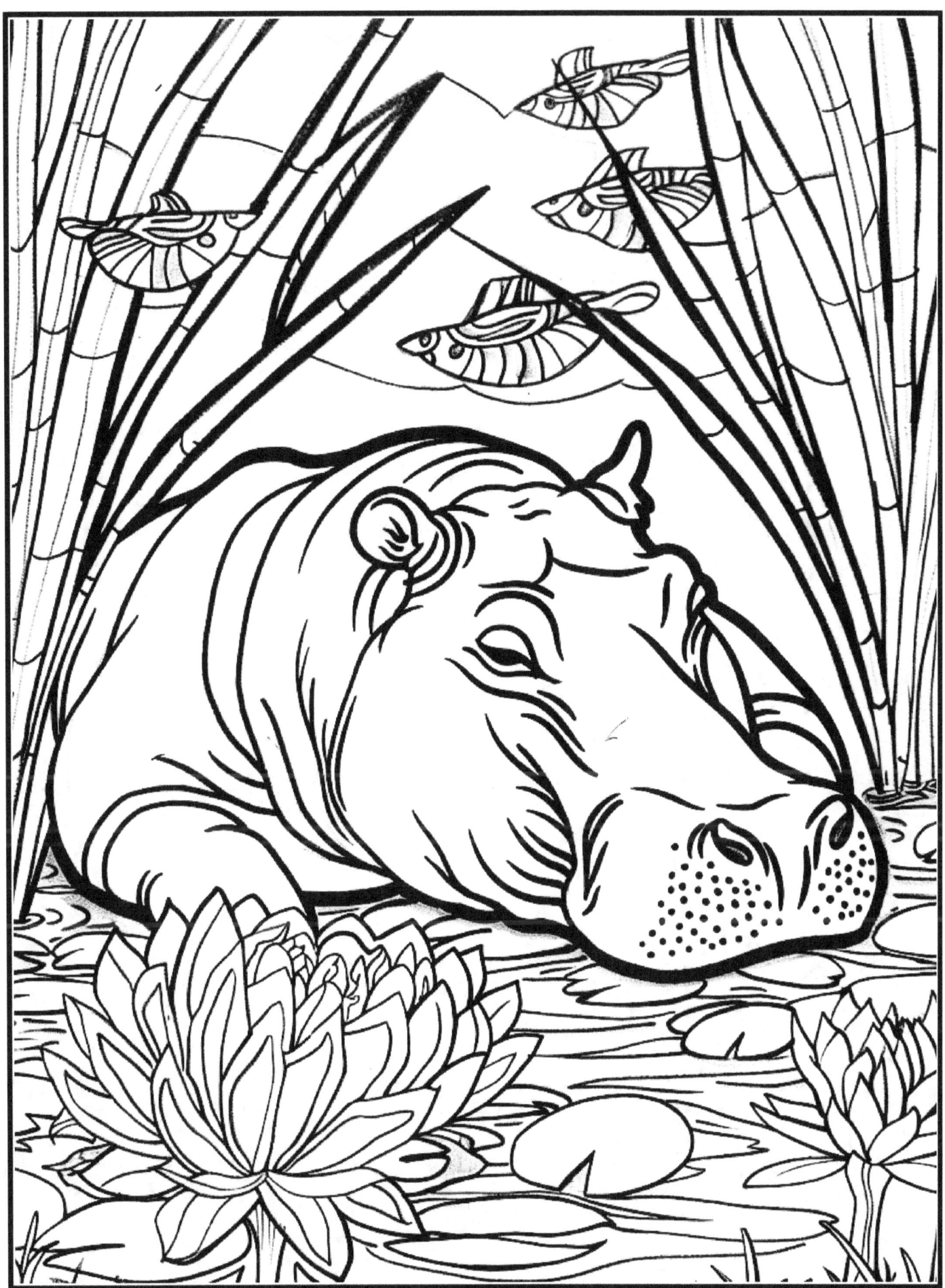

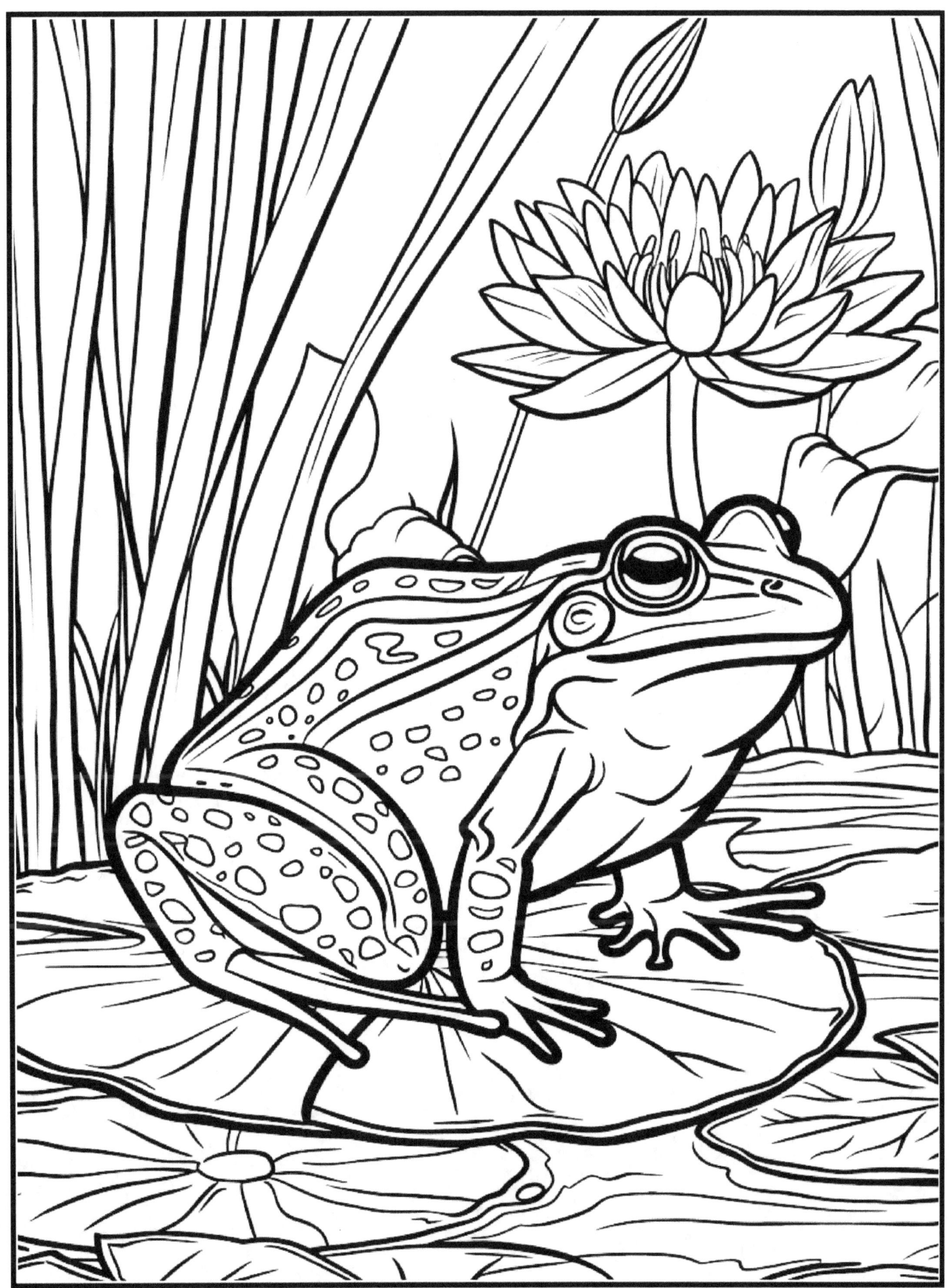

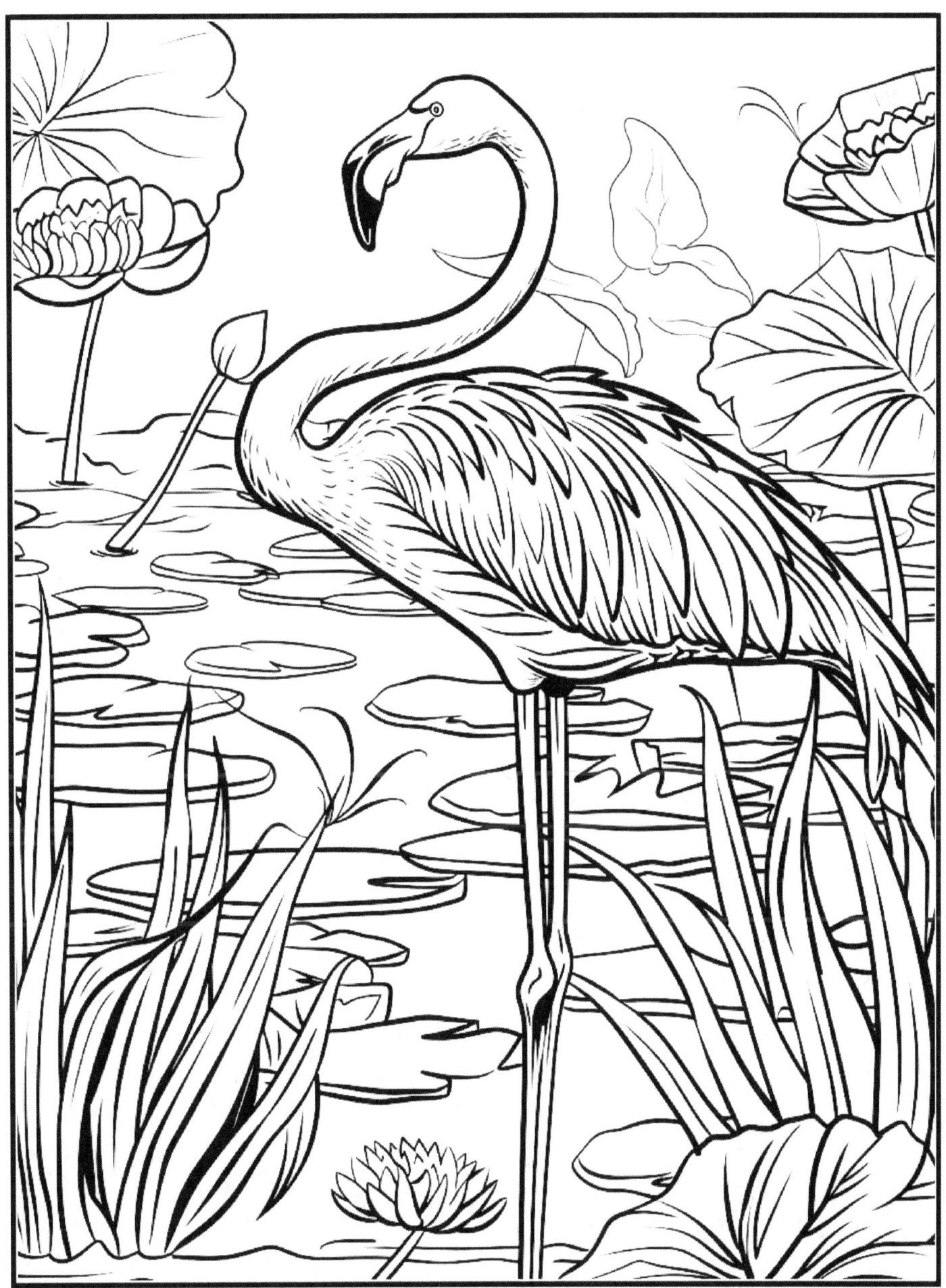

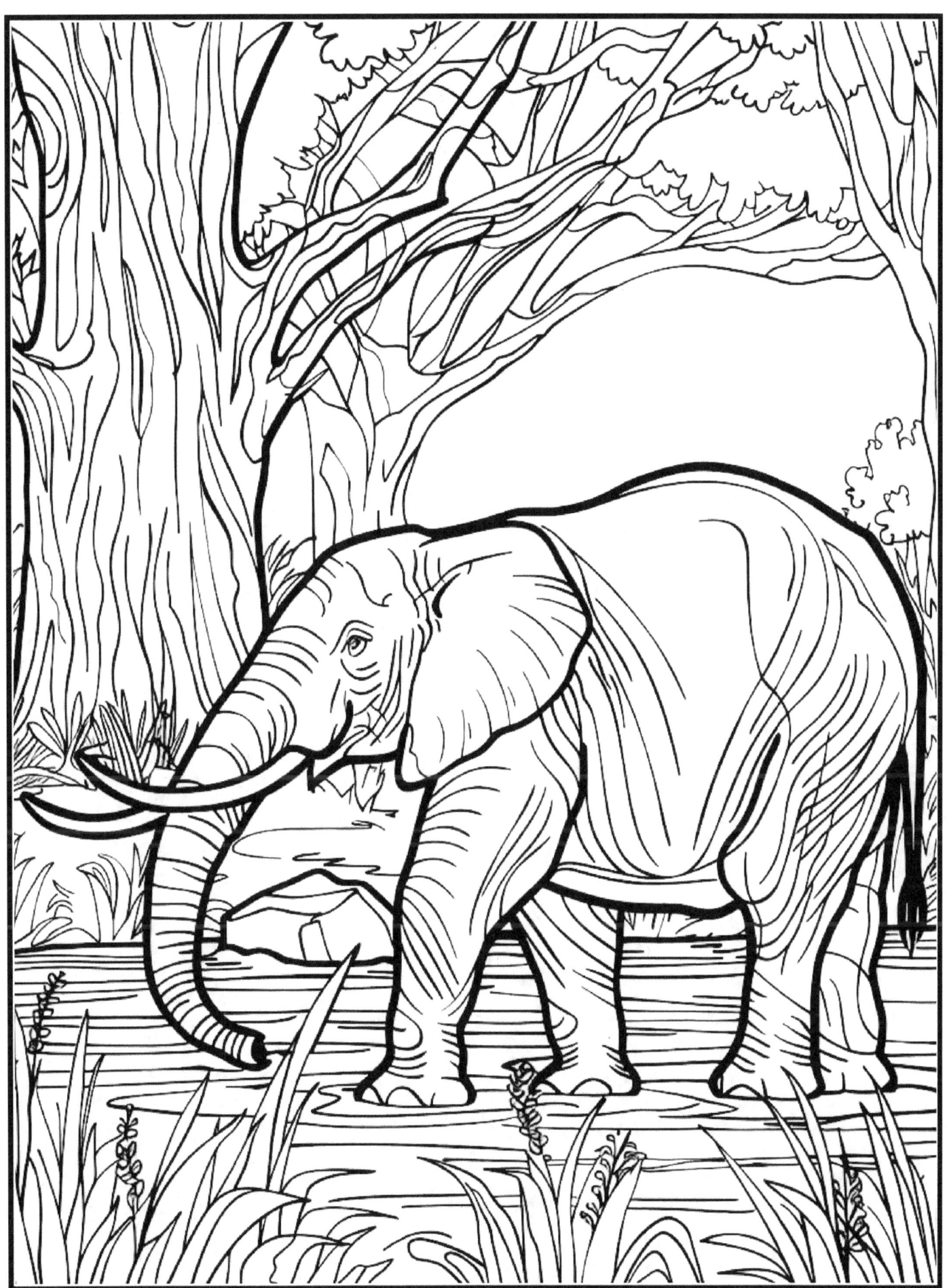

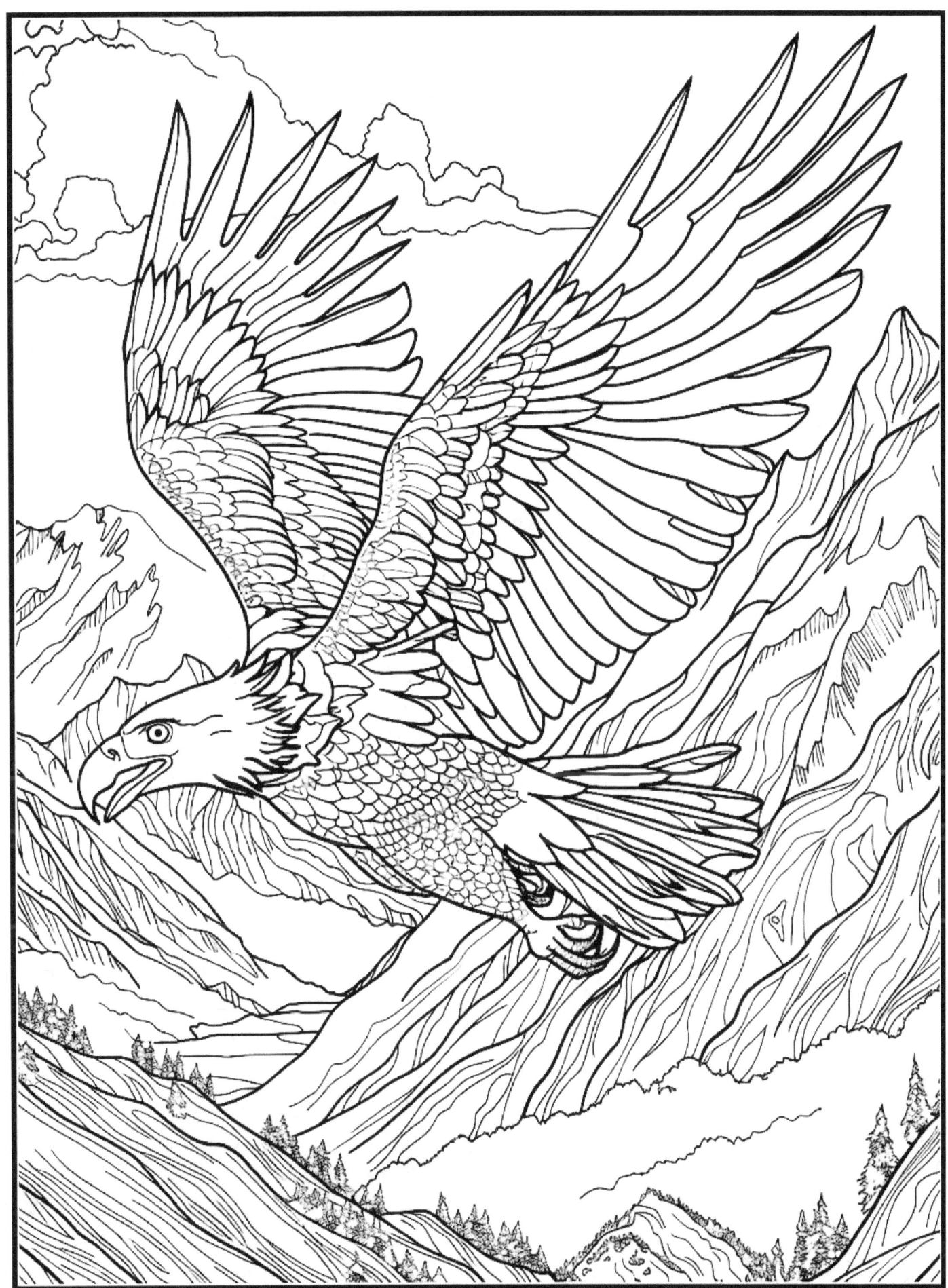

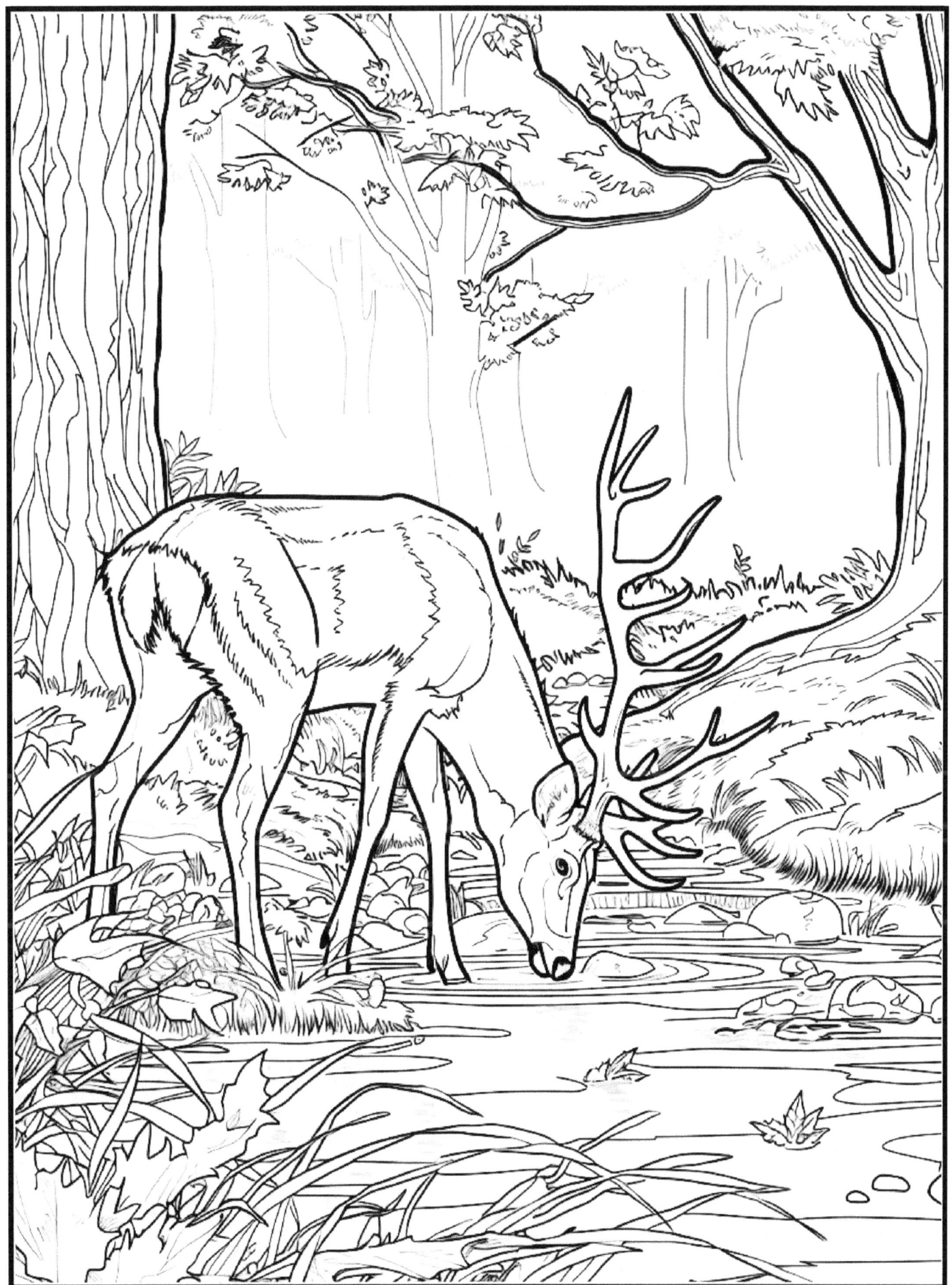

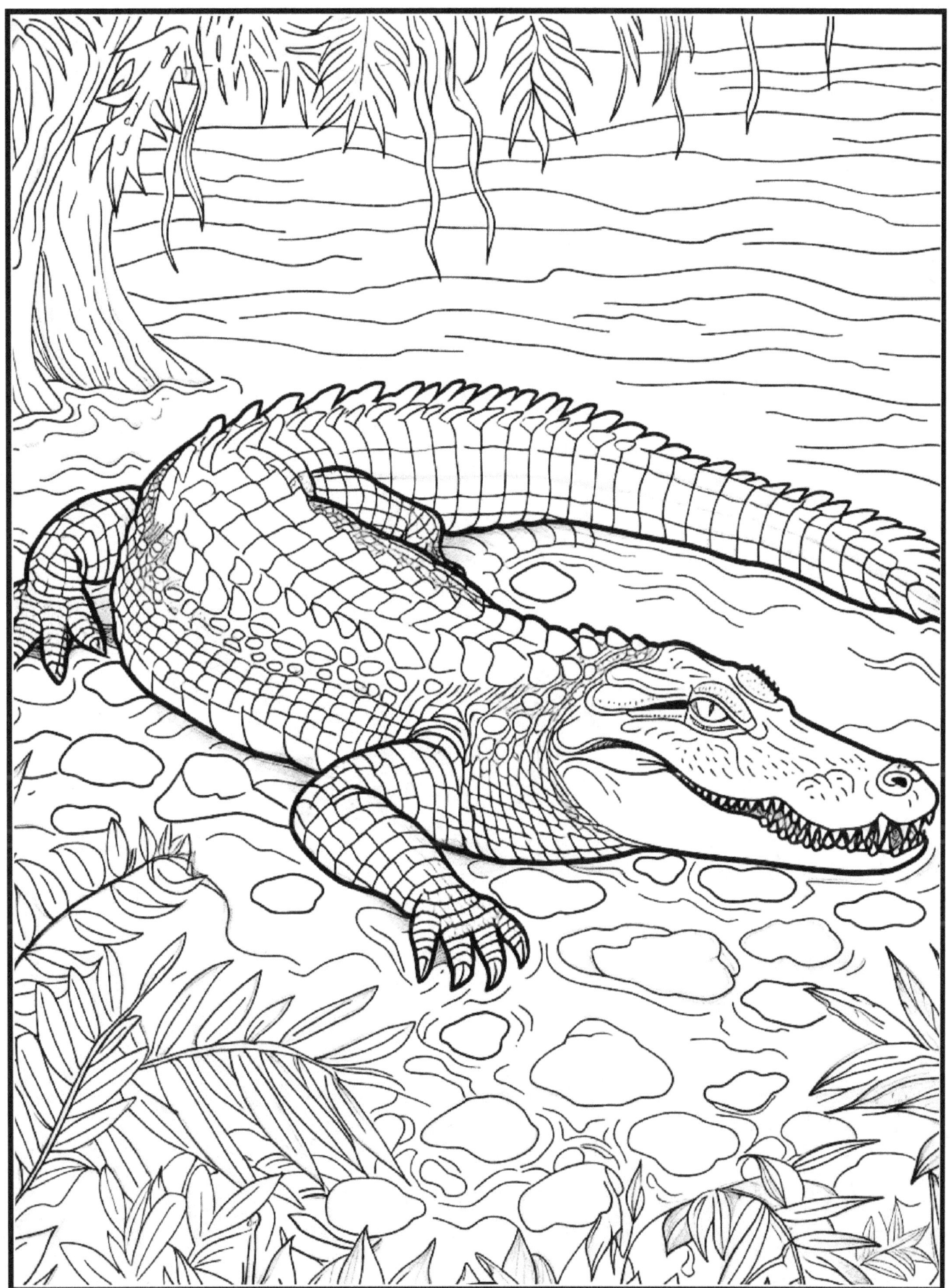

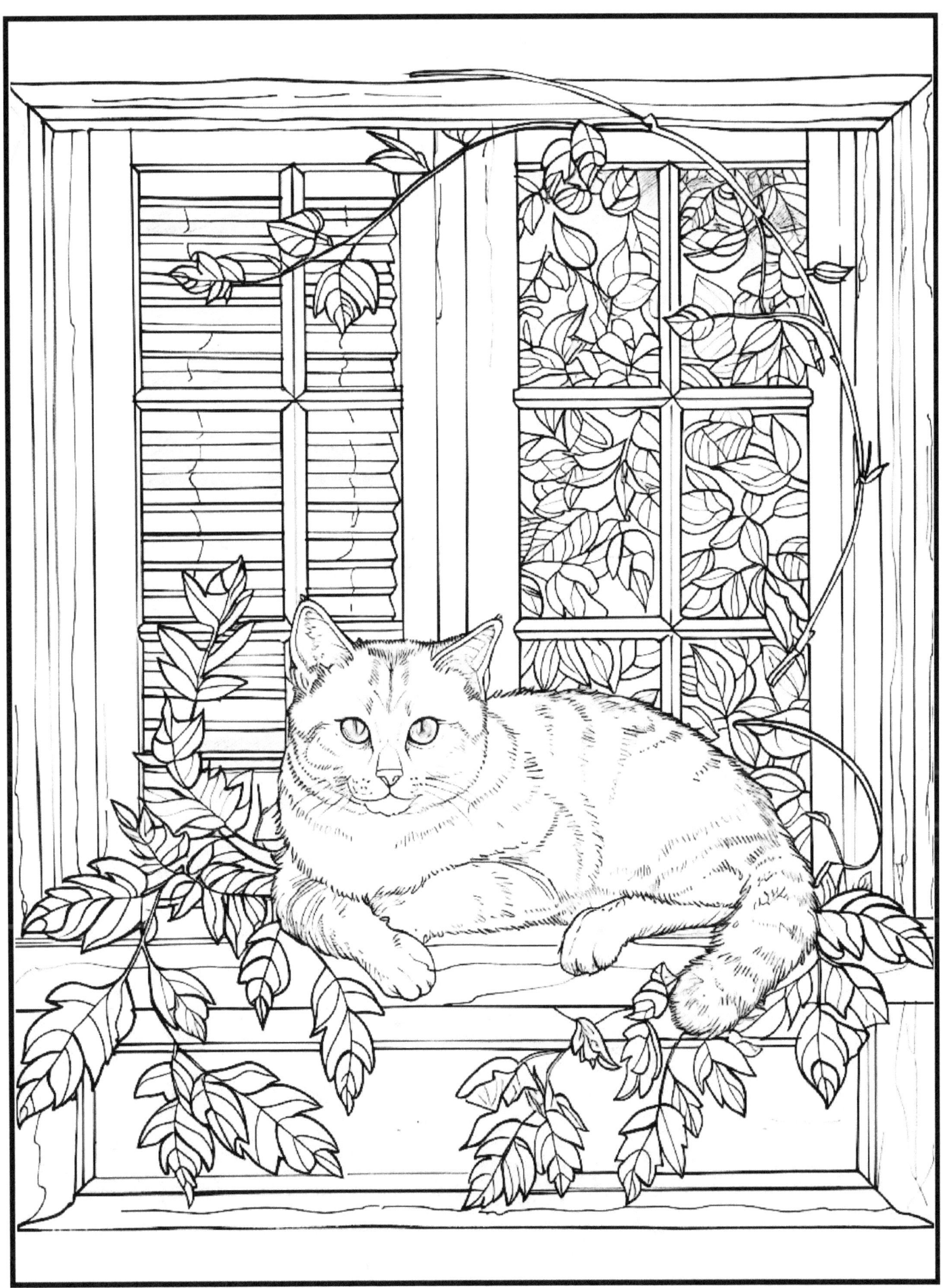

www.ingramcontent.com/pod-product-compliance
Lightning Source LLC
Chambersburg PA
CBHW082221220526

45470CB00010B/3256